THE LAST PRINCESS

THE STORY OF PRINCESS KA'IULANI OF HAWAI'I

FAY STANLEY · ILLUSTRATED BY DIANE STANLEY

HarperCollins*Publishers*

KAUA'I
ISLAND

NI'IHAU
ISLAND

For my daughter — again. — F.G.S.

For my mother — again. — D.S.

Special thanks to Naomi Noelani Chun of the Kamehameha Schools,
Hawaiian Studies Institute, for her critical reading of this text.

Grateful thanks to the University of Hawaii Press for permission to adapt
a portion of the *Hawaiian Dictionary,* by Mary K. Pukui and Samuel H. Elbert
(Honolulu, Hawaii: 1986 edition), in the note on the Hawaiian language.

The text of this book is set in 14-point Pegasus.
The illustrations are rendered in gouache.

The Last Princess. Text copyright © 1991 by Fay Grissom Stanley. Illustrations copyright © 1991 by Diane Stanley Vennema. Printed in the
United States of America. All rights reserved. First published in 1991 by Four Winds Press. Reissued in hardcover by HarperCollins*Publishers*
in 2001. Published by arrangement with the illustrator. www.harperchildrens.com

Library of Congress Cataloging-in-Publication Data. Stanley, Fay. The last princess : the story of Princess Ka'iulani of Hawai'i / Fay Stanley ;
illustrated by Diane Stanley.   p.   cm.   Originally published: New York : Macmillan, 1991.   Includes bibliographical references (p.).
ISBN 0-688-18020-5 — ISBN 0-06-029215-6 (lib. bdg.)   [1. Kaiulani, Princess of Hawaii, 1875–1899—Juvenile literature.   2. Princesses—
Hawaii—Biography—Juvenile literature.   3. Hawaii—History—Juvenile literature.   [1. Kaiulani, Princess of Hawaii, 1875–1899.   2. Princesses.
3. Hawaii—History.   4. Women—Biography.]   I. Stanley, Diane, ill.   II. Title.   Du627.17.K3 S73   2001   996.9'028'092—dc21   00-32048
[B]   CIP   AC   1   2   3   4   5   6   7   8   9   10

THE HAWAIIAN ISLANDS

Hawai'i is made up of a chain of 132 islands, with eight
main islands in the southeastern end of the chain.
The island of Hawai'i gives its name to the entire group.

O'AHU
ISLAND

Honolulu area —

MOLOKA'I
ISLAND

PACIFIC   OCEAN

LĀNA'I
ISLAND

MAUI
ISLAND

KAHO'OLAWE
ISLAND

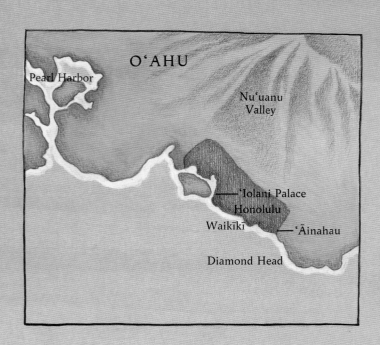

O'AHU

Pearl Harbor

Nu'uanu
Valley

'Iolani Palace

Honolulu

Waikīkī   'Āinahau

Diamond Head

HAWAI'I
ISLAND

Mauna Loa

The life of Princess Ka'iulani of Hawai'i began like the happiest of fairy tales. She was the only child of the beautiful Princess Miriam Likelike and her wealthy, handsome husband, Archibald Cleghorn. And she was the first child born to the royal family, for her uncle, King Kalākaua, had no children of his own. From the day of her birth on October 16, 1875, Princess Ka'iulani seemed destined to become queen of this ancient island kingdom.

At the news of her birth, all of Hawai'i rejoiced. Bells rang joyously from church towers. Cannons fired noisy salutes. Hawaiians hugged one another and wept with happiness. An heir to the Hawaiian throne had at last been born!

The precious baby was christened on Christmas Day. Her mother, Princess Likelike, chose a name for her that was almost bigger than the tiny infant herself. As the priest sprinkled holy water on her doll-sized head, he baptized her Princess Victoria Ka'iulani, Kalaninuiahilapalapa Kawēkiu i Lunalilo. The name Ka'iulani means "the royal sacred one."

Artist's imagined portrait of the royal family at the time of Princess Ka'iulani's christening:

FRONT ROW, LEFT TO RIGHT: Queen Kapi'olani; her husband, King David Kalākaua; his sisters Princess (later Queen) Lili'uokalani and Princess Miriam Likelike Cleghorn; and, held by her mother, Princess Victoria Ka'iulani   BACK ROW, LEFT TO RIGHT: Princess Ruth Ke'elikōlani, governor of the island of Hawai'i and Ka'iulani's godmother; husband of Princess Lili'uokalani, John Owen Dominis, governor of the island of O'ahu; Princess Likelike's husband and father of Princess Ka'iulani, the Honorable Archibald Cleghorn (later governor of O'ahu)

The baby's aunt, Princess Ruth, who had a great and generous heart, was named one of her godmothers. As a christening present, she gave little Kaʻiulani ten acres of land in Waikīkī. This beach on the island of Oʻahu was once the meeting ground of Hawaiʻi's warrior chiefs. There, the princess's father built his family a fine new house. He called it ʻĀinahau, which means "the cool place," because of the fresh breezes that blew down from the mountains. Around the house, he created the loveliest garden in all that beautiful island.

Archibald Cleghorn came from Scotland. Though he was a commoner, not a member of a royal family like his wife, he was a wise friend and advisor to King Kalākaua. A successful importer, he was also an expert in the art of growing plants and flowers.

At ʻĀinahau, he planted sweeping emerald lawns bordered by royal palm trees. In front of the house stood a majestic banyan tree, which became a favorite play place for little Kaʻiulani. He imported spice trees from India with scented bark that perfumed the air, and eight varieties of mango trees to provide delicious mango chutney for the princess's table. Then he added bright-blooming hibiscus and dense thickets of trees with exotic names like monkeypod, ironwood, camphor, buttercup, and breadfruit.

Every day Kaʻiulani played there with her giant turtle and hand-fed the peacocks that strutted across the green lawns. She often rode her white pony, Fairy, over the beautiful grounds or went surfing or swimming off Waikīkī. Another child might have been spoiled growing up at ʻĀinahau, but the princess was a sweet-natured, merry child adored by family and servants alike.

When she was older, she began lessons in the cool, dark house with her governess. Ka'iulani did well in her studies and was said to be as bright as she was beautiful. It was not until she was eleven and her mother suddenly became ill that the first dark shadow slanted across the little princess's life.

During Christmas of 1886, Princess Likelike was not her usual lively self. She grew quiet. Then one day she suddenly refused to eat anything at all and took to her bed.

Likelike was clearly dying. Although she seemed to have no known illness and her husband brought one doctor after another, the princess grew weaker and weaker. In February of 1887, at the very end of her life, Likelike sent for little Ka'iulani.

Those who were there said that the room was darkened and a faint smell of medicine hung in the air. Princess Likelike seemed to be sleeping. But as Ka'iulani approached, her eyes opened and she stretched out a pale hand to her only child.

Then with a voice so low that Ka'iulani could scarcely hear her, she whispered that for a moment she had been allowed to see into the future. She paused for breath, then told the child what she had seen: "You will go far away from your land and your people and be gone a very long time. You will never marry and you will never rule Hawai'i."

Later that afternoon, Princess Likelike died, and Princess Ka'iulani's storybook childhood came to an end. But despite her sorrow, she was brave and self-controlled, and she went on with her studies and royal duties. As an *ali'i* — a noble from the revered ruling family — she had been taught to set a good example for her people.

Ka'iulani was now the next heir to the throne, after her Aunt Lili'uokalani. When she was fourteen, the king and queen and her father decided that she should be sent across two wide oceans — the familiar Pacific and the forbidding Atlantic — to a boarding school in England. There, she could receive an education fit for a future queen.

At the thought of leaving her father, her friends, and her beloved Hawai'i, Ka'iulani was very grave. Though she tried to hide her feelings, she had a new friend who sensed the sadness in her heart. He was an enormously tall Scotsman, ridiculously thin, with dark, watchful eyes. His name was Robert Louis Stevenson, the author of *Treasure Island, Kidnapped,* and other great stories for children.

Stevenson was spending a few weeks in Hawai'i and had become friends with all the royal family, but especially with the little princess. He described her as "more beautiful than the fairest flower." He would sit with her under her gnarled banyan tree and spin tales of his travels, or tell her stories about the little mouse who visited him in his grass work shack whenever he played his flute.

When the time for Ka'iulani's departure drew near, Stevenson wrote a special poem for her in her red plush autograph book. It began:

> Forth from her land to mine she goes,
> The Island maid, the Island rose,
> Light of heart and bright of face,
> the daughter of a double race.
> Her islands here in Southern sun
> Shall mourn their Ka'iulani gone,
> And I, in her dear banyan's shade,
> Look vainly for my little maid.

In May of 1889, Kaʻiulani boarded the S.S. *Umatilla* to leave Hawaiʻi for the first time. As the ship left Honolulu Harbor, the band began playing the national anthem, *"Hawaiʻi Ponoʻī."* Sadly, Kaʻiulani waved good-bye to the crowds that had come to see her off, then continued to wave and wave until the last tiny speck of green disappeared from sight.

The voyage across the Pacific Ocean was rough, and Kaʻiulani was seasick most of the time. As the princess's ship neared San Francisco, the weather grew colder. She had never felt cold before and was chilly even bundled up in heavy clothes.

But worse than the cold was having to say good-bye to her "Papa" in San Francisco. Here, she boarded a train with friends for the long journey across America. Kaʻiulani was awestruck at the size of the country, and when she finally reached New York, she was dazzled by the tall buildings and the throngs of people and carriages in the streets. In New York, she boarded another ship to cross the Atlantic Ocean, where she was miserably seasick again all the way to far-off London, England.

In September, Ka'iulani left London for her school, Great Harrowden Hall. This elegant three-hundred-year-old mansion was now a private school for the daughters of rich and royal families. The princess met with many new things there. The cold. The discipline. All the other girls. And the classes themselves — for she had never been to a real school before!

Despite all the strangeness and her lingering homesickness, Ka'iulani soon made many friends, and she enjoyed her classes. She studied French, German, English, history, music, and the social graces that she would need when she became queen. During school holidays, she traveled in England and Europe. She attended balls and parties in London and house parties at great estates in the English countryside. And she frequently visited her guardian, Theo H. Davies, a family friend who lived in England and looked after the princess when she was there.

Her letters from this period are happy and carefree. They show her interest in the ordinary things that affected ordinary girls of her time. She wrote of problems with German verbs and of having to wear spectacles for her nearsightedness. She chattered on about clothes and friends and flirtations and of exciting plans being made to have her presented to Queen Victoria at court in the spring.

But from time to time, in letters arriving from Hawai'i, Ka'iulani came to learn about more serious things. From friends and family, she heard more and more about politics and problems at home.

Even though the Hawaiian islands looked like tiny specks on a map, they were important to other countries because they were located right in the middle of the Pacific Ocean. What a perfect place for ships to get fresh water, fuel, and supplies when traveling to the Orient! What an ideal spot for traders to swap Oriental goods for American and European products. What a handy place for a military base. And what fertile land for raising rich crops to sell cheaply to other parts of the world.

For all of these reasons, the governments of Britain, France, Russia, and the United States had for years battled with one another to take over the islands — either by force or by trying to influence her kings to do whatever they wished. By the time Ka'iulani was in England, a certain group of successful businessmen was really running the government.

These *haole* (Hawaiian for "foreigner") men were mostly white Americans. Many of them were sons of the missionaries who had come in the early 1800s to bring Christianity to Hawai'i. The missionary families generally felt superior to the Hawaiians. They were openly scornful of their religion. They couldn't recognize the intelligence of a people whose culture was so different from their own. They called the Hawaiians "savages." And because these families thought themselves so much better than the Hawaiians, they believed they were doing them a favor by telling their kings what laws to pass and dictating who could vote and who could not.

Over the years, this group of Americans had grown rich and strong. By marrying into noble Hawaiian families and by tricking innocent farmers out of their land, they owned vast ranches and sugar cane plantations. Some became wealthy merchants and traders, and so gained control of shipping, banking, and politics.

The *haoles* had become so powerful that in 1887, they had forced Ka'iulani's uncle, King Kalākaua, to accept a new constitution that took away some of his ruling powers and said only some of his people could vote. Although the *haoles* — who were not even citizens — could vote, most of the Hawaiians could not because they were poor and without property.

In letters from home, Ka'iulani now heard that the *haoles* wanted to annex Hawai'i to the United States, which meant that America would completely take over her country. This was upsetting, but it did not prepare her for a shocking message she received in October 1890 from her uncle, the king. At the end of an otherwise normal letter, she read a chilling sentence warning her to *"be on guard against certain enemies I do not feel free to name in writing."*

Puzzled and frightened, Ka'iulani wrote back asking the king to speak more clearly. But there was no reply. Two months later, she received a cable saying that he was dead! Suddenly, Ka'iulani's "Aunt Lili'u" was queen and Ka'iulani herself was next in line for the throne.

Aunt Liliʻu was in many ways a stronger ruler than her brother had been. Since the *haoles* could not control her, they decided to overthrow her instead. On January 16, 1893, a company of American marines marched into Honolulu.

This show of force was all that was needed. The sight of the marines encamped near ʻIolani Palace convinced Liliʻuokalani that she must give up the throne as the *haoles* demanded.

It was two weeks before Kaʻiulani learned of this revolution. Friends said later that she never fully recovered from the blow. But her kindly guardian suggested that there might still be a way to save her kingdom. She must go at once to Washington and personally speak to the new president, Grover Cleveland! Only he could block the planned annexation of Hawaiʻi.

Kaʻiulani was dismayed at the suggestion. She was only a timid seventeen-year-old. How could she presume to single-handedly oppose the powerful *haoles,* or influence the president of one of the greatest nations on earth? But in spite of her terror, her love for her country and her people made her reconsider. "Perhaps some day the Hawaiians will say, ʻKaʻiulani, you could have saved us, and you did not try,'" she told her guardian. "I will go with you."

Once she had decided on her course, Ka'iulani did not waver from it. Before leaving England in February, she spoke of her cause to newspaper reporters and won their hearts completely. A few weeks later, when she and her guardian docked in New York, she conquered the American press, too. The reporters wrote about her delicate beauty, her talent for music, art, and languages, and her manners—those of a "born aristocrat." And when she read her short, prepared statement many had tears in their eyes.

In a quiet voice, she told the reporters how it felt to arrive alone "upon the shores ... where she thought to receive a royal welcome" to find enemies working to take away her kingdom, to "leave her without a home or a name or a nation." She finished by saying, "Today, I, a poor, weak girl with not one of my people near me and all these ... statesmen against me, have strength to stand up for the rights of my people. Even now I can hear their wail in my heart and it gives me strength and courage."

When Ka'iulani finally arrived in Washington, President and Mrs. Cleveland were deeply impressed by her courage and dignity. The president assured the princess that he would see justice done to her and her people. He announced that a special investigator would sail to Hawai'i immediately to report on the true situation there. This was the happiest news Ka'iulani had received since the revolution. Believing she had successfully accomplished her mission, she felt free to return to England.

But after the hectic month in the United States, it was hard for Ka'iulani to settle back to her schoolgirl routine. She waited anxiously for news from home. It finally came in August. The president's representative was back from Hawai'i and had reported to the Senate that a "wrong had been done to the Hawaiians, who were overwhelmingly opposed to annexation." The president then urged that Congress find a way to restore the queen to her throne.

It seemed to Ka'iulani that she had won. She, "a poor, weak girl," had helped save her aunt's throne and her people's independence. But her joy and triumph at the good news was short lived.

The *haoles* refused to disband their new government, and the president was unwilling to send American troops to force the *haoles* to step down. The only help he could give the Hawaiians was to block their country's annexation as long as he was president.

A group of outraged and disappointed young Hawaiians decided to take matters into their own hands. If the United States government could not restore their queen, they would do it themselves — by force!

For months, these fiery young men planned their revolt. They secretly shipped in guns from California, which they buried on the beach at night. On the evening of January 6, 1895, they gathered together and prepared to storm Honolulu the next day. But because a spy in their group told the authorities about the plan, and because the young men were poorly trained and armed, they were quickly put down. About two hundred Hawaiians were arrested, among them many friends and relatives of Ka'iulani's.

To save the lives of these revolutionaries, the queen agreed to sign a document in which she formally gave up the throne. But the queen's punishment was not complete. She was also imprisoned in her own palace, tried for treason, and given a sentence of five years at hard labor plus a fine of five thousand dollars!

Later, this savage sentence was lightened. But the monarchy was finished. Hawaiian kings and queens would never again rule over their beloved people.

In these last years, many Hawaiians had been robbed of their land and their right to vote, and now they had lost their own government. They were now a minority in their own country, outnumbered by immigrants from the Orient and the *haoles.* White man's diseases had caused the death of many of these independent, good-hearted people.

At the bitter news from Hawai'i, Ka'iulani put aside her own dismay and grief and thought of her people. She knew in her heart that her place now was at home.

When Kaʻiulani's ship arrived in Hawaiʻi on November 9, 1897, the biggest crowd ever assembled at the Honolulu docks was there to greet her. Through tears, she received them aboard ship, then let herself be driven through an Oʻahu she scarcely recognized.

Everything looked different. The people were downcast and ragged. ʻIolani Palace seemed tiny after the great palaces of Europe. At ʻĀinahau, the vegetation was so dense that she scarcely recognized the estate. And the new mansion her father had built for her in her absence was so grand and unfamiliar that she could not feel at home in it.

But Kaʻiulani would not let herself dwell on used-to-bes or might-have-beens. She was there to help her people. In the months after her return, she tried to do all that was expected of her. She kept her poise and dignity, but refused to be drawn into politics, setting an example to all Hawaiians during this time of heartbreaking change.

After President Cleveland left office in 1897, Congress voted to annex Hawai'i to the United States. The formal Annexation Day came on August 12, 1898. At 'Iolani Palace the band played *"Hawai'i Pono'i"* for the last time and the Hawaiian flag fluttered to the ground. But Ka'iulani was not there to witness it, nor were most of her people. The islands were in mourning. Houses were shuttered across the land. Ka'iulani sat alone under her banyan tree. She heard the guns from warships in the harbor boom out and knew Hawai'i's time as an independent nation was over. It was said that she quietly wept.

During the following months, Ka'iulani avoided Honolulu, hating the sight of the American troops everywhere and the sad faces of the Hawaiians. In December, glad to be away, she attended the wedding of her friend Eva Parker at the fabled Parker Ranch on the island of Hawai'i.

The wedding party was so large that it overflowed several houses and so gay that it lasted past Christmas. In mid-January, while horseback riding with friends, the princess was caught in an icy downpour. All the others pulled on raincoats. But Ka'iulani suddenly swept off her hat, shook her hair loose from its neat bun, turned her face to the storm, and recklessly galloped off in the driving rain.

The next morning she was feverish, and every day afterward she grew worse. Ka'iulani's father arrived to take her home to 'Āinahau, where she lay ill for weeks. The doctors called her illness inflammatory rheumatism, but some thought her real disease was despair.

Ka'iulani drifted in and out of consciousness. Sometimes she opened her eyes and smiled at friends and family gathered around her bed. Early in the morning of Monday, March 6, 1899, she stirred, cried out, then grew still. Witnesses said that at the moment she drew her last breath, her peacocks in the darkness outside began wildly screaming their almost human cry.

Hawai'i was plunged into mourning. All day Wednesday, thousands of weeping Hawaiians filed past Ka'iulani's casket at 'Āinahau, then clustered together under the banyan tree, wailing ancient Hawaiian funeral chants. Even more of her people marched in the torch-lit procession that took her body to Kawaiaha'o Church at midnight. They spoke in whispers, and even muffled the hoofs of the horses pulling the hearse.

For over three days, Ka'iulani lay in state at Kawaiaha'o Church. Following her huge and beautiful funeral on Sunday, she was at last taken to the Royal Mausoleum in Nu'uanu Valley. Bells pealed and cannons roared, just as they had when Ka'iulani was born. Twenty thousand silent and stricken Hawaiians watched as Ka'iulani passed by for the last time.

After only twenty-three years, Princess Kaʻiulani's role in Hawaiʻi's history was over. As Likelike had foretold, she had traveled far and had been long away from her people. Although many young men had adored her, she had never married. And, finally, she had never been queen.

Or had she? She spent tireless years in exile and study to fit herself for her royal duties. She fought bravely in Washington to preserve the freedom of her people. She endured loss and sorrow with noble dignity. Perhaps the last princess of the little Hawaiian kingdom was indeed a queen.

PAU
(FINISHED)

A Note on the Hawaiian Language

The Hawaiian alphabet has twelve letters: five vowels (*a, e, i, o, u*) and seven consonants (*h, k, l, m, n, p, w*). To pronounce Hawaiian words properly, it is necessary to know the rules for pronunciation and to see how the words are written with their *diacritical* marks.

Diacritical Marks

There are two diacritical marks: the *glottal stop* (ʻ) and the *macron* (ˉ). These marks show how a word is pronounced and help to indicate the correct meaning of the word. (Hawaiian words may be spelled with the same letters, but will have quite different meanings depending on their pronunciation. For instance, the word *pau* means finished, ended, or completed, while *paʻu* means soot or smudge, *paʻū* means moist or damp, and *pāʻū* refers to a woman's skirt.)

The glottal stop appears only before or between vowels. It indicates a break in the voice, like the sound you would make in saying "oh-oh." Words in this book that use the glottal stop include *Hawaiʻi* and *Kaʻiulani.*

The macron is used only over vowels and indicates that the vowel should be stressed, or emphasized. The macron can also change the vowel's pronunciation. Words in this book that use a macron include *Kalākaua* and *Waikīkī.* (Some words, like *ʻĀinahau,* use both the glottal stop and the macron.)

Vowels

Hawaiian words contain many vowels. Every word or syllable ends in a vowel, and *every* vowel is sounded.

Unstressed	Stressed
a like a in about	ā like a in car
e like e in net	ē like ay in day
i like y in city	ī like ee in bee
o like o in pole	ō like o in pole (same as unstressed o)
u like oo in moon	ū like oo in moon (same as unstressed u)

In the following vowel combinations, the first vowel is always stressed: ae, ai, ao, au, ei, eu, oi, ou.
In one vowel combination, both vowels are stressed evenly: iu.

Consonants

h, k, l, m, n, and p sound about the same as they do in English.
w: after i and e, usually sounds like v
after u and o, usually sounds like w
at the beginning of a word and after a, can have either a v or w sound.

BIBLIOGRAPHY

D'Anglade, M. G. Bosseront. *A Tree In Bud: The Hawaiian Kingdom, 1889–1893.* Honolulu: University of Hawaii Press, 1987.

Daws, Gavan. *Shoals of Time: A History of the Hawaiian Islands.* Honolulu: University of Hawaii Press, 1968.

Day, A. Grove. *Mark Twain's Letters from Hawaii.* New York: Appleton-Century, 1966.

Day, A. Grove, with Ralph S. Kuykendall. *Hawaii: A History, From Polynesian Kingdom to American Commonwealth.* New York: Prentice-Hall, 1948.

Gillis, J. A. *The Hawaii Incident, An Examination of Mr. Cleveland's Attitude Toward the Revolution of 1893.* Freeport, N.Y.: Books for Libraries Press, Reprint 1970.

Loomis, Albertine. *For Whom Are the Stars?* Honolulu: University of Hawaii Press and Friends of the Library of Hawaii, 1976.

Mrantz, Maxine. *Hawaii's Tragic Princess — The Girl Who Never Got to Rule.* Honolulu: Aloha Graphics and Sales, 1980.

Mullins, Joseph G. *Hawaii Journey.* Honolulu: Mutual Publishing Company, 1978.

Rayson, Potter Kasdon, with Norris W. Potter and Lawrence M. Kasdon. *The Hawaiian Monarchy.* Honolulu: Bess Press, Inc., 1983.

Stevenson, Robert Louis. *Travels in Hawaii.* Honolulu: University of Hawaii Press, 1973.

Tabrah, Ruth. *Hawaii: A Bicentennial History.* New York: W. W. Norton & Co., 1980.

Tate, Merze. *The United States and the Hawaiian Kingdom, A Political History.* New York and London: Yale University Press, 1965.

Webb, Nancy, and Jean Francis. *The Hawaiian Islands, From Monarchy to Democracy.* New York: Viking Press, 1956.

_____. *Kaiulani, Crown Princess of Hawaii.* New York: Viking Press, 1962.

Zambucka, Kristin. *Princess Kaiulani: The Last Hope of Hawaii's Monarchy.* Honolulu: Mana Publishing Co., 1982.